More Shadow than Bird

NUAR ALSADIR's poems and essays have appeared in numerous periodicals, including *Grand Street*, *The Kenyon Review*, *Ploughshares*, *Slate*, *The Awl*, *AGNI*, *Tin House*, *Lit*, *Gulf Coast*, *Ribot*, *The New York Times Magazine*, and *Book Forum*. When not writing, she teaches at New York University and is training to become a psychoanalyst.

More Shadow than Bird

Nuar Alsadir

SALT

LONDON

PUBLISHED BY SALT PUBLISHING
Acre House, 11–15 William Road, London NW1 3ER, United Kingdom

© Nuar Alsadir 2012

The right of Nuar Alsadir to be identified as the
author of this work has been asserted by her in accordance
with Section 77 of the Copyright, Designs and Patents Act 1988.

Salt Publishing 2012

Printed and bound in the United States by Lightning Source Inc.

Typeset in Swift 9.5 / 13

ISBN 978 1 84471 887 0 paperback

1 3 5 7 9 8 6 4 2

For Isadora & Sabine

Contents

Acknowledgements

Grateful acknowledgement is made to the following journals and anthologies in which some of these poems have appeared:

AGNI Review: "Absinthe," "Breakfast," "Man on an Island."
The Awl: "Morning."
Callaloo: "Sing Fat."
Fine Madness "On the Ride Home from Mourning."
Grand Street: "Chiaroscuro, "The Renovated Room," "Two Years" (as "Untitled").
Gulf Coast: "What Is Denied."
The Kenyon Review, "Aperture," "Bats," "Deposit," "The Garden."
Lit: "Disquiet."
Passages North: "Walking with Suzan."
Ploughshares: "Caesura's Palace."
Poetry Daily: "Caesura's Palace."
Slate: "The Riddle of the Shrink."
Tin House: "The Closet."
Broken Land: Poems of Brooklyn: "Walking with Suzan."
Inclined To Speak: Arab American and Diaspora Literature: "Bats," "The Garden," "The Riddle of the Shrink."
Saudi Aramco World: "Chiaroscuro."
Post Gibran: Anthology of New Arab American Writing: "Agyrophobia" (as "Aftermath"), "The Window's Oven."

The author would like to thank The Fine Arts Work Center in Provincetown, Yaddo, The MacDowell Colony and Ledig House International for their generous support. The author would also like to thank Daron Hagen, whose setting of "Congedo" was both recorded on *Love in a Life: Eight Songs for Voice and Piano* and included in his collection of sheet music entitled *Songbook*.

More Shadow than Bird

Still Life with a Bedroom on an Airshaft

A neighbor's light switches on in a window
across the airshaft, absorbs the darkness
like a person eager to speak.

There's a grainy stillness to all,
as though the sleepers had been painted,
as though they became what the painter

layered over in shifting focus
from the couple to the unspoken,
which slips like a mouse between dreams.

You'd have to take a step back to see them:
up close they are nothing more than a cluster
of syllables, your name, what you say

when the only words you hold are stones
that were thrown against the window
of your childhood fears while you pretended to sleep.

Unknown Knowns

The crow in the yard warns *go — go —*
like the flock above Hatches Harbor

flapping *jibe ho —* & thwacking inland
to take position before the storm.

My daughters sit near the window,
hear the crow without hearing,

play a game of call & response: *rah,*
says one, giggling, then the other, *rue;*

a secret language of foreboding
already inside them — & growing —

The Exile's Letter

A piece of the exile's letter broke off
into my hand. Li Po, I am sorry.

Ez Po, too (it was your translation).
I walk the underground, thinking

The dead are on my lips—
they speak in grains, small syllables,

many instruments like the sound
of young phoenix coos—

but nothing from the ashes.
Their speech is self-extinguishing,

impressionistic: you get close
and nothing makes sense.

What is the use of talking! And there is no end
to talking, there is no end to things of the heart.

On the other side of the mottled pane
the mourning dove sits hatching her brood,

more shadow than bird, like a falling-off
from a first world, meiosis of light.

An age is gone.
It is the darkness that is divisible.

Deposit

Water falls and leaves itself
like blood in the basin, staining.

That is when I remember, go out
of the silence I've created

as a mouth unfolds to open
when mimicked by the hand.

A name is another imitation,
tumbling across centuries,

a bud detached from stem.
The past returns beheaded—

gone, gone, my blooming.

Bats

They live inside walls—not like you
or the other rodents, but with wings

and fangs, a clicking almost flamenco.
And unlike you, they are not ashamed:

they share their darkness like a piece
of delight and when the circling begins

do not feel their minds invert.
You, crawlers, guard your flight,

may swim the air in dreams
but always rise for breath, belief.

The bats do not need applause.
If you clap, they will change direction.

The Garden

There is no garden, there never was.
The man who cuts the grass is stealing,

making promises with his Miracle-Gro
and reeling in the fish. I want to believe

in something: each morning I look out
at the patches, squint until they turn green.

Are you with me, wherewithal?
I am everywhere without.

A garden is a mood: this one less
of disciple's brood than drought.

Imago

Sometimes you find someone gone from your life
has entered your unconscious the way a piece

of a toy breaks off, gets lost in the center
and rattles around at certain angles of movement.

He slides imperceptibly through the mind
yet always appears with the same slanted thought:

the message his presence, the weight of things,
how it must be determined anew.

Insufficient Moon

The many shapes of moon shuffle through phases
like a child's flip book of animation.

I turn to the night's chapter—sliver,
then gone—and am not satisfied.

One must have the mind of the faithful
to turn to the trees; to read in spaces

between leaves vigilant things,
yet watch them ascend night like decoration.

Augury

The crow knows,
hangs under the sky
with accusatory inflection.

Wit gathers
and is gone from me:
I grow spectral, imitate stone.

Smoke rises
from the mission next door.
A man without a cup paces, starves.

The Riddle of the Shrink

It's the distress of losing a ticket
or any other document granting passage.

When the phone disconnects
just as you were about to be let in

on a secret, you become the letter
that never receives a response, the ball

that rolls under the neighbor's fence and stays.
The friend you have entrusted with your death

song, an editor, has changed the words.
Now it's you, not your modifiers,

who will dangle, suspended between this world
and the next. The image of the future

is the memory of the dream in which
you're standing before a kiosk, attempting

a transaction with a forgotten code.
The more you talk, the more you're left alone.

At times, you're curious whether or not
someone is in the room, but fear it would be

too revealing to check. At times, you strain
to hear another's conversation while feigning

involvement in your own. When the subway doors
open and everyone rushes to take a seat,

you're trying to get over to the right lane
in fast traffic. It's like wearing tights

with a stretched-out waistband under a skirt,
or dreaming that the alarm is about to go off.

Hemophobia

I cannot bear the sight of blood,
so when I saw some in the tub

I thought maybe my husband was dying.
I asked him where it came from

but the question only annoyed him.
He said he was late and stormed

out of the house in a summer suit.
It was January. I could not stop him.

Agyrophobia

Today I felt happy for a moment
on the corner, but the sky backed its bookbag

into the crossing & blocked my light.
Where there had been joy was static.

Everyone was upside down & falling out
like change. Sometimes it seems there was never

a time before: a truck pulls in front
of your crossing & there is no tomorrow;

your hat flies off & suddenly you're facing home;
the man rushing by who bumps you

is your father, his strange eyes crackling
you don't belong here —

                              but with a blink
it's he who has gone.

Cremnophobia

Our silences, simultaneous,
overcrowd the void—

in the dream, I'm seated
at a banquet, eating.

A man and a woman squeeze behind me,
push my body to the seat's precipice—

such as it was to sleep in the same bed
with him, perhaps also the cat.

Hypegiaphobia

We are descending again in parallel—
I cannot say together—as in another dream

you rushed through the first door
without me. It was late. Your name

was an elevator door resisting its rail,
its screech my only attempt to reach you.

Was it the hurt that filled the elevator
I entered with gurneys and gowned girls,

incubated hearts pumping for a home?
Floors flicker as they fall.

The girls' chatter flaps shrill at light,
tangles in my hair and away

like spring, like spring—
      When the doors open

you will be on the other side, waiting,
mistaking my elation for rage.

Gametophobia

The stutter was fixed;
man behind one door,
woman on the fence;

an old dictionary
split in two,
all words after "I"

under the couch
until movers came
and it was time to marry.

Caesura's Palace

I sat on the sofa staring at the plant
now growing more upright and asked him

to recite a poem. Excitedly, he popped up,
pulled a yellowed paperback from the shelf

and handed it to me as though he were
making a hole in the sand for my chignon.

The reeds waved like swords in the wind.
My stockings came off like surprised fish

and I—
but he broke off, took the book from me,

placed it back on the shelf and returned
our glasses to the kitchen.

All was dissolved with the putting away
of objects, his spatial *Well then—*

Two Years

It takes two years to pass through a house.

I sit and let my hair grow,
grow all around me
like morning or plague.

Between rooms, dark
corridors, unmarked graves.

I hear the onion
in their shouts, crying,
they call to me.

I, with no way,
the blink in my heart heavier
than a dove's feather.

No matter.

Shut your door.
You whose grasp
strangles and thaws,

shut your door.

The Renovated Room

All white, symmetrical. My eyes
fly across walls with greed:

forgotten nail, where paint
has peeled. Memory tumbles

in the spirit of stairs, phrase
or word in infinite recede:

the mind a palimpsest, Chaplin's
hat hopping at every reach.

The Closet

About to spill, the shape
of man, it opens. The soul,

in its many blouses, waits.
Gravitational or otherworldly,

I don't know which thrust makes
relative of wood. And of shoe,

a lower beauty: anima not in
whole, but right relation to foot.

Absinthe

Like this are the days
and like this the nights

but the mornings they are different,
early afternoons.

I'm counting the ways you comfort me
like a soldier counts his legs.

In these altitudes
I forget to breathe.

I am the broken plate
over and over.

You come to me straight,
double into aside.

I'll never be here,
my throat full of night.

You sit across from me,
going blind.

Man on an Island

What cries overhead is bird. I had wanted
to go where I wouldn't be scared;

so much uncertainty in a sky held up
by words and smog. But there is nowhere

enough for me—I who have
no lungs, who have no true.

The sky has stopped loving me; it falls
in pieces of snail and dew. It is the same

wherever I go. The trees lose their leaves,
some fold like birds exhaling,

and the branches stand proud
in empty letters, but I—

I can't bear the words, don't want the wind
or beak, sucking in my own *caaaww*

caaaww. The ocean at night is uglier
than your eyes when they close.

]
]
noise protects the silence
like a decoy
]

The Messy Apartment

So this is what it becomes,
what all becomes in the end:

pieces, dread, and the only
way out to go in again.

Mess is the male of anguish.
O small rue covered by sock,

lint, penny unspent! All morning
the hollow has been deepening,

the falter brought out.
It beckons through a cold-kept

season: relentless, clattering,
dragging slog-caked boot into night.

Aperture

I close the wardrobe, it opens.
I close the wardrobe, it opens.

Is that the way it will always be,
persistence as a form of flight;

my summons the rising and slamming tight
though rust will gather despite me?

I've folded my dresses, placed them
on shelves. I could affix

another hinge, but the walls
have become a cluster and repetition

a way to light—to light
through the absence it exposes.

The Streetlight

One night, window cracked, she spoke.
She, with hair tied into horn. *Without walls*

the world is a lodging, she said,
locks slipping to absorb night's fray.

As opposed to a house or a thing forgotten? I asked,
considering how she came: through window,

through sleep. *Let us think of ourselves,*
how we destroy ourselves everywhere.

Chiaroscuro

I'd seen it in moments,
rat-light scampering then slid,

but never this: shadow relieving
light; the edge of forgotten;

a flatiron, the single sliver
stretching into tenement,

many stories, room into
room; a way to give.

The Window's Oven

God cooks food outside the house,
my grandfather tells me when he comes

from the dead to see me off in a dream.
I am running with my bags, afraid

of missing a flight. They fall one
then the other, come undone.

The floor spreads to sky beneath me,
stirring the colors of my clothes into white:

the after image of solitude stoked
into hunger-steam and all it ignites.

Insomnia

The wall hangs the hour.
I've catalogued my losses,

ground them into pills.
Each falls to the earth like sleep,

an infant's tilted face.
The park, the snow, the park erased.

]
]
]my head heavy
like February
or wet wool
]

Morning

when dark, is not that,
morning, but more like rain:

a sky of smog-stuck potatoes,
frustration without eyes.

The way I did nothing exhausted me:
I fed the wall,

ran water over my body
until it swirled down the drain.

On a determinable plane
I am undetermined,

on a moving train,
unable to find a seat.

The edge is what knows me,
the face half-carved out,

the gutter that gathers its objects
like knives, without connection,

here what is not there and vice versa.
I lie. I have seven jars of lies:

one for each day and the joy!
of repetition. Weeks redouble

and hold me still, anchors sprout
from my feet, stand in for will.

Desire is the lie I tell on Tuesday.
I tell it with my socks off

to be understood. The color
of intent is the crispness of bread;

whoever wants the heel
comes last to the table.

What if Charlie Parker was Picasso and my face were made of sound?

Breakfast

The eggs taste different today
and everyone is crying.
Especially me, we are all crying.

Her teeth are white and she's wearing
all white. He thinks she's a trail
of cigarette butts to something human.

Then she moves. We all start over again.
Morning. We crack eggs in the pan,
wait to see what creature will rise.

He's tattooing Jesus on his arm, a loaf
of bread and the devil. The three demands
are getting confused. Let me try a proof:

I am a woman and I am not a man.
I am not the woman, I am not the man.
Hopeless. The eggs taste different today.

Morning. He keeps following and looking
through her. She's angry. He doesn't notice,
she's not the path, but where it begins.

What Is Denied

Everything tastes like dog,
the sun won't come up
and the neighbors are hiding behind their doors.

I walk from my bedroom to my kitchen
which is my bedroom
but still I am hungry.

Will the dream's caul now be denied to me?
The fatty film, the kiss
that tastes like sapphire and stains my knees?

What about the pocked door,
orange man, jelly on the hand
that won't wipe off?

These bricks turn their walls on me,
a car alarm preaches abstinence
in four ways like a Pre-Raphaelite painting

saying *this, marry like this*
so the girls cross their legs
against the cuckoo throb of spring.

The Ride Home from Mourning

My underwear is in my backpack
and I feel true—it is impossible

to elaborate. Accuracy, said Hume,
is advantageous to beauty. So I say,

grey, with thin strings. I love
the morning when it is cold,

and I and Amtrak cut through ice.
Outside, the land rises to pass:

it is the mother, the grandfather,
all the gods and their children.

Where do we go when we go
no more? The unmooredness puzzles.

I want a language that replaces every "or"
with "and," that decides for us whether

to connect or dress. Connect and dress:
this is what we do when we mourn,

the unintelligible inside us
and the accurate on our backs.

Disquiet

The days have been cold and the windows leak. It is winter and I don't want it.

I feel it like the loss of arms. The space around me is different. There exist invisible planes we stand on and mine have shifted. I feel a change in gravity, in the way I sense the world.

First Avenue: eyes closed, arms spread, everything passing out of me —

Death came wearing an ugly shirt.

What distracts is not the same as what feeds. My tea tastes like something I can't identify. Or is it my mouth that tastes?

Feeling ineffectual: a terrible thing.

I wrote a letter and it felt like carrying a heavy suitcase up three flights of stairs: I ran with it, eyes closed to the strain. It's a question of presence, not being able to settle into anything, the scatteredness, the inability to be.

What blooms does so in the space that breaks from knowing.

Beauty blooms from a state of imbalance. Yet, when is one in a state of useful imbalance, and when is the self ghosting—the soul standing next to the body instead of inside it?

I never wake hungry. I must not have rolled into this world a hungry body. But I know desire: the split between what is and what is wished. Everything desired rests together on a plane, creates a world the wanting opens into. Desire bends backwards, into the self. It has nothing to do with the world.

If I love something I want to lick it or bite it. Thrust my body against it to wrap around its shape. I want to be the shape of things I love.

I'm suspended above my bed like fever. There's a door below called Terrible Way, but I only half see it.

I keep looking at the building on 13th Street. Balconies stick out like feeders on a bird cage, all lined vertically. Could it be that the cage is the outside, the unmarked space rather than the walled-in?

My neighbor's cough: I hear it through the ceiling; I hear it from the stairs. It hurts my entire body.

Finding a way to live historically and unhistorically: doing the dishes while you cook.

Other people can never influence the mode of your feeling. They spur emotions as a neurotransmitter does, binding and setting off a reaction. But the neurotransmitter itself doesn't do anything, it just binds. Others can be the right shape to bind to a synapse, but the emotion they spur was already inside you. It's completely yours.

I'm stuck, again, in the back of the morning.

I fear I'll fling myself at the feet of strangers who pass; then, as when sick, draw comfort from the cold ground against my face. That doesn't happen: the flinging, the comfort. Nothing but the same day turning inside out and stuffing into the same pocket.

Reason is like light, it comes in quanta. There are no lines connecting thoughts, only packets and leaps.

Letting-be, a rigorous self-gathering.

First Street. Rain. The bus pulls up like a surfacing whale. We're conditioned to think of a horizontal move as a surfacing up. It's just a horizontal move, from Second Avenue to First, the difference what's sold there.

]
]
The umbrella snaps back with a fast click
like the visual *tsk* of a brow raised in consternation
]
I should be home with my dissertation—
]
]

Aurelia in August

Black omphalos this waiting.
Where are you?
Body an umbrella, a bell,

shielded from effulgence
I lurk in a craze-enclosed ringing,
a jelly-like hell.

Octatic my eyes,
yet unable to see, I shrink
into imagined horrors and swell—

numb, numb this jealousy.

Jane E.

Face down, sleeper, hide your fists.
Bertha angers at your door.

All day locked and something
madly wrong, you rise nightly

with your guilt, toss, hover
where the garret begins,

at the bottom of her call.
Drink cleared her escape,

Grace's flask her path to you,
the key drunkenness let fall.

Io

Forsaken. This was not choice,
but horns and hooves become you.

Strange to all, you feed their stares.
Clucks catch in fur. For the one

who left another came: you look
into his eyes but they are many.

Where is he, the one who said,
Do not be afraid and ravished?

Loveless one, in despair
you shall be learned —

desired, you inhabit deception.

Congedo

These days extend—like holes
in stockings, they extend—

Love, have I mentioned my melancholy?
You become that in your absence.

In presence you break: morning light,
running radio to water to coffee

and cleaving in clank, saucer
to spoon like rest only upward.

I come to you that way. But you—
you pace: your many hallways one room

in the center a table where we drank.
This is not your moment. Ahead

or behind, you dwell out of skin,
rest the sorrowful folds before me.

It is late last night the door was shut over fire
and the one not home misspelling his name in sleep—

It is you are the hull of this undesire
and the self-simulations it bespeaks—

Guest

Your mother's in the kitchen and out
and in again. It's all about them.

They've taken over like the dark cloud
hanging low over the back yard,

a fat aunt coming in for a hug.
Enough's enough. The door opens:

new guests flow in as the old
back you up like mangroves.

Why get dressed up to stay in?
Pretend to befriend other children

because they have been dumped next to you?
Resistance, then fire, then to your room

without toys. Later, it'll be the boys
to whom your friends will cater,

seem to love best. Such is the fate
of the steadfast: you'll never be a guest.

Trees at Night

Trees at night: black black,
shadows I believe in, smoke

that won't disappear. Edges
rise into sky then fall,

blur half way between hope
and recollection; the cat out

the window and back again,
knowing passage through return.

In the distance, cars erode
the highway, seashell to ear,

but east or west they go on,
children in backseats sleeping.

Walking with Suzan

We hear a sound like a mammoth door
creaking open. She tells me it's a woodpecker,

and I imagine that little nose opening worlds.
I think of hearing a poet read a few weeks ago;

sitting in the front row I wanted nothing more
than to touch his nose. I told this to my friends

at Pete's Tavern after the reading and someone
called it sweet. Jeff would probably call it sublimation.

I start talking with Suzan about how difficult it is
to marry appearances with intention and she wants

to walk around what looks like mint but could be
poison ivy. My mother used to grow mint

in our backyard; we called it by its Arabic name, *nànà*.
A few years ago, I learned the English word

for *tukie* is *mulberries* and *ramane* is *pomegranate*.
I have spent my life confusing words, mixing up

what I mean with what I say. The other day
when we were lying on my kitchen floor and I said

you should go, I could have said *I'm scared*
or *help me believe*. But there is little to believe in

since what we see is not necessarily out there
and language hollows being into desire.

Even when I try to talk about what I want I start to lie.
There's a lot to be said for walking around things.

Still, there are times when a skeptic tries,
a woodpecker banging itself into a tree.

Sing Fat

I will not write another love poem, I decide,
passing the Sing Fat Restaurant on 3rd and 12th.

Who but Whitman could do that, *sing fat*?
It's like Williams dancing around naked

while everyone's sleeping, or Vallejo
wanting to kiss affection on its two cheeks.

Yesterday, I was explaining to my fourth graders
why we say *Native Americans*, how it's important

to call people by names they choose, and Sarah Bliss
told me she wants to be called *Beautiful Girl*.

My mother used to call me *Little Boy*
because that's what I wanted to be; I'd watch

my brother melt the heads off his army men
and think, *what power!* Now I sit at a desk,

drawers filled with tape and Kleenex,
answer questions like why there is no willn't

if there's a wouldn't and a couldn't.
We talk about what colors we would be,

how happy endings are an adult conspiracy,
and how they don't like another teacher

because she's like paper. Last night I dreamt
I was pregnant, which is supposed to be a good omen,

but I sprinkled salt on my stomach and watched
the baby shrivel like a leech. If I could accept

what comes, I'd be dancing naked, bulging with life,
finding no sweeter fat than sticks to my own bones.

Notes

Reference is made to the following authors and works:

The Exile's Letter

Lines 13–14: "What is the use of talking! And there is no end of talking—/ There is no end of things in the heart." Pound, Ezra. *Cathay* (London: Elkin Mathews, 1915).

Imago

Lines 7–8: "What do you believe in?—In this: that the weight of all things must be determined anew." Nietzsche, Friedrich. *The Gay Science*, ed. Bernard Williams (Cambridge: Cambridge University Press), p. 152.

Io

Lines 9–10: "Loveless one, in despair you shall be learned." Roethke, Theodore. *Straw for the Fire* (Garden City: Doubleday, 1972), p. 151.

Salt American Poets

Bruce Andrews
Robert Archambeau
Shaindel Beers
Charles Bernstein
Maxine Chernoff
Matthew Cooperman
T. Zachary Cotler
Catherine Daly
Joe Francis Doerr
Rachel Blau DuPlessis
Jamey Dunham
Aaron Fagan
Annie Finch
Cherryl Floyd-Miller
Benjamin Friedlander
Forrest Gander
Peter Gizzi
Loss Pequeño Glazier
Andrew Grace
David Hamilton
Henry Hart
Jerry Harp
Brian Henry
Nathan Hoks
Anselm Hollo
Paul Hoover

Lisa Jarnot
Katia Kapovich
Hank Lazer
Rebecca Lehmann
William Logan
Aaron McCollough
Jill McDonagh
Jennifer Moxley
Philip Nikolayev
Geoffrey O'Brien
Michael O'Brien
Ethan Paquin
Jared Randall
James Reiss
Mark Rudman
Mark Salerno
Susan M. Schultz
Don Share
Ron Silliman
Alan Sondheim
Jared Stanley
Nathaniel Tarn
Anne Tardos
Terry Ann Thaxton
Catherine Theis
Susan Wheeler

Lightning Source UK Ltd.
Milton Keynes UK
UKOW04f0826010915

257870UK00004B/123/P